RUTH

Finding Grace in the Unexpected

A 4-WEEK STUDY

MARIEL DAVENPORT

GOD HEARS HER | Our Daily Bread Publishing.

Requests for permission to quote from this book should be directed to: Permissions Department, Our Daily Bread Publishing, PO Box 3566, Grand Rapids, MI 49501; or contact us by email at permissionsdept@odbm.org.

Published in association with Mary DeMuth Literary, mary@marydemuthliterary.com.

Interior design by Michael J. Williams

ISBN: 978-1-64070-423-7

Printed in the United States of America
25 26 27 28 29 30 31 32 / 8 7 6 5 4 3 2 1

CONTENTS

INTRODUCTION

Every part of life involves transition. Growth, development, milestones, and changes are constants in life. As I box up things from my firstborn's room for his move across town, I'm reminded of my need for stability in all the changes. My son's upcoming wedding, my other son's approaching graduation from college, our move to a new town, the passing of my dad—all mark transitions in my life, places where I need to be reminded of God's grace.

As you consider your own life's transitions, I wonder where you have anchored yourself in their midst. Our God is a rock for us, our stronghold. I find myself returning to a familiar place in the Bible when I near major changes in my life, as I search for grace in the unexpected. God spotlights a woman in Scripture who—despite experiencing loss and the unknown—held fast to the One who held her fast.

Ruth is a woman who knew transitions well. She buried her husband; moved to a foreign land; was the caregiver of her bitter, widowed mother-in-law; and even navigated the adjustments of a new marriage and motherhood. In some ancient Jewish traditions, the book of Ruth appears directly following the book of Proverbs; its proximity to Proverbs leads some scholars to believe that Ruth was considered the living embodiment of the Proverbs 31 woman! (Both women are also described by the same Hebrew word—*chayil* [meaning "valor"]—and they are the only women to receive this commendation.[1])

In other Jewish traditions, the book is placed preceding the Psalms as a recognition of the book's connection to King David. David, the author of most of the psalms and a key figure in Israelite history, is a great-grandson of Ruth. In the English translations of the Bible, the book of Ruth is placed following the book of Judges in a concern to follow chronological and historical order.

Ruth has profoundly influenced my own relationship with God. As a new wife and mom and someone new to faith in Jesus, I yearned for the example of a godly woman, and found it in Ruth—in her character and in her surrender to God. Her account in Scripture has taught me that I too can find grace in the unexpected, and so can you.

My Atheist Eyes Opened

As a young woman who had been an atheist, I surrendered my life to Jesus after reading Genesis in a Bible borrowed from a coworker. Unsure what the Bible held in its pages, and in an attempt to guard my insecure heart, I approached Scripture with skepticism. The challenge before me was to disprove the Bible.

One evening as my newborn lay asleep and my young husband sat watching the news, I opened the Bible for the first time. Never could I have imagined what would happen in the days ahead as I continually returned to the complicated storyline of dysfunctional people in Genesis—to whom I could relate all too well! My eyes were opened! Every day at work, I peppered my coworker with questions, and she never seemed to tire of sharing the gospel with me. By the reading of the last chapter of Genesis, I surrendered my life to this one and only God who had given His perfect Son for me.

This newfound faith in God filled me with excitement, joy, and a bit of hesitation since I was completely green in my knowledge of the Bible. As a new wife and mom—and a first-generation Christian in my family—I had trouble finding older women to mentor me along the way. Maybe that's why the book of Ruth caught my attention early on. Ruth is an example of lived-out godliness. Her character compelled me to uncover her story in Scripture and, even more so, to seek to know and trust her God.

The book of Ruth is set in the time of the judges, when "everyone did what was right in [their] own eyes" (Judges 21:25). We also navigate life in a culture where everyone is doing what is right in their own eyes. As masterfully illustrated in the brief book of Ruth, God is at work redeeming and wooing His people despite the corruption and injustice of the time. As women of God and of His Word, we, like Ruth, can choose to trust Him as we uncover God's unfailing character revealed in the Bible. God will prove Himself faithful to you and me just as He did for an ancient Moabitess.

Tending Your Soul

As we lean in to learn from Ruth, it can feel intimidating to approach the Scriptures, and even more so, to rightly live in response to it. After many years of living dependent on other people's Bible studies, I yearned to hear God's voice through His Word for myself. I studied how to dig into the Bible inductively, which is a practice of observing and seeking to rightly interpret the text based on the context before applying it to your life.

As I sat in my backyard salsa garden and learned to tend the young plants there, God taught me how He desired to tend my soul by His Word. In the process, the TEND method was born and has been my guide through Scripture for many years. TEND is a simple, meaningful inductive approach to discovering God's Word. TEND encourages us to slow down and listen carefully to the heart of God and to draw near to Him.

As You Begin

Just as a gardener gathers her tools before heading into the garden, you will want to gather yours. All you will need:

- *Your favorite Bible.* Having access to various translations on a phone or laptop can be helpful too.
- *Pen or pencil of choice.*
- *This guided journal.* Throughout the journal, there will be some suggestions for further study; some of these resources are listed in Appendix B. These resources are extra and certainly not *needed* to begin tending your soul by the Word. But they are helpful for digging deeper as you grow in your study of the Bible.

How to Use the TEND Method

TEND is an acronym that guides you through a simple four-step method to engage with God's Word for yourself. (To learn how to TEND through a Bible passage, scan the video podcast QR code on page 9.)

- **T** stands for ***Take time to pray***. As you begin the study, simply pray and ask the Holy Spirit who teaches us truth (John 14:25–26) to lead and direct your mind and heart as you uncover His Word.
- **E** stands for ***Examine the Scriptures***. Write down the verses from the day's directed Bible text. (Need help with choosing a translation? Check out Appendix A.) As you copy down God's living words, consider the subjects and verbs in the verses. Place yourself in the scene.
- **N** stands for ***Notice the lessons***. Rather than jumping to application, we want to pause here to consider what the author was saying to the original reader or hearer of these words. Ask yourself, *What is being taught here? Is there a characteristic of God being revealed?* Then write out the attribute of God displayed. This step will take practice, but the time and effort are worthwhile because the goal of time in the Bible is to know and love God more. That begins by identifying what the verse is teaching about God.

- **D** stands for ***Do what it says***. We want to be doers of the Word, and not hearers only (or readers only), deceiving ourselves, as James 1:22 warns against. In this final step of TEND, we want to respond to what God is teaching. Consider the insights from Scripture in light of your own life, your relationships, and your circumstances. How will you respond to who God is and to the lesson you gleaned today through your relationships or circumstances?

  Some days you might respond by praising God, repenting, or journaling. Other days you might respond by texting an apology to someone or encouraging someone the Lord brings to mind. We will never look like Jesus if we have a head full of learning but lack applied knowledge. If that's the case, we will remain weak-willed and increasingly vulnerable to the enemy (2 Timothy 3:1–7).

New to the TEND method? Join me, using the QR code below.

SETTING THE CONTEXT

Looking at the background and context is imperative as we prepare the soil of our souls to walk with God through Ruth, the only Old Testament book of the Bible named for a non-Israelite woman.

1. What Genre Is This Written In?

The book of Ruth is a historical narrative, meaning it is the retelling of the actual events that happened to the family of Elimelech.

So where in history does this story happen? Knowing the metanarrative of Scripture helps us understand the book of Ruth's purpose and meaning within the larger scope of Scripture.

According to Impact 360 Institute, "The metanarrative is the big picture of the Bible. Though it is essential to take a deep dive into specific pieces of scripture and meditate over them, it is easy to forget that the Bible is one big story of a family. It begins with Adam, leads to Jesus, and continues through us."[1]

The metanarrative of Scripture:

Creation → Fall → Redemption → Consummation

Exploring the Metanarrative of Scripture. **Creation** happened at the beginning of time as outlined in the first chapters of Genesis. The **fall** of humanity followed when Adam and Eve chose to sin against

God, ushering sin into the world and damaging our relationship with God. Before the fall, Adam and Eve had direct access to their Creator. Consequences of Adam and Eve's sin included their removal from the garden of Eden and loss of constant communication with Him. Still, God pursued humankind, foreshadowing the direct access to Himself that He would offer in His Son, Jesus.

Jesus would reconcile humanity back to God. Born of a virgin and without sin, Jesus Christ was sacrificed in the place of God's people at the cross, which brought **redemption** for those who would trust in the Messiah Jesus. Jesus was then resurrected. He returned to heaven to sit at the right hand of the Father. He also sent the Holy Spirit to indwell those who surrender to Jesus until the day of **consummation**, when God's people will be eternally together in His presence.

Between the fall in Genesis and Christ's redeeming sacrifice in the New Testament were many ups and downs for God's people, including the period we will be focusing on. Just before God assigned them a king in the book of 1 Samuel, the Israelites were led by judges.

Ruth: When the Judges Ruled. Around 1100 BC, during the rule of one of the judges, a severe famine in Israel affected the land in and around Bethlehem, which means "house of bread."

In the book of Ruth, a young family from Bethlehem sought pasture for their dying flock and thus traveled as far as the land of Moab. Moab was across the Dead Sea from Bethlehem. The area had been founded by Abraham's nephew Lot and his family under sinful circumstances (see Genesis 19:30–36). The people of the area were known for their worship of Chemosh and other pagan gods.

As mentioned in the introduction, during this time, "everyone did what was right in [their] own eyes" (Judges 21:25). The period of the judges was a season of heightened moral anarchy. When God's people returned to the promised land, the Lord raised up judges to lead His people. Those judges often failed to lead the people in righteousness and led them away from God.

The book of Judges highlights the cycle of rebellion and idolatry among God's people. When the Israelites rebelled against God, they were subjugated by other nations. In their oppression, they cried out to God and He would raise up a judge to deliver them. After their deliverance, the Israelites served the Lord for a time, until they didn't. Again. Forgetting God's goodness to them, they would return to other gods. The final verse of Judges (see above) illustrates a vivid picture of what was going on then, and what is common to us in our human nature: rebellion, enslavement, cries for rescue and mercy, deliverance, gratitude, and right back to rebellion.

Have you noticed this cycle in your own heart in the seasons of your life? What a gift grace is! When we come to God and confess our sin and rebellion, God offers us the grace through Jesus that we desperately need (1 John 1:9).

2. Who Wrote the Book?

The Jewish Talmud credits the prophet Samuel as the author of both Judges and Ruth, though the author is never disclosed in the text itself.

3. To Whom Was the Book Written?

The original audience of Ruth was the Jewish people.

4. When Was This Book Written and When Did Its Events Occur?

The book was likely written around 1000 BC to 962 BC, during the time of King David's reign, which is why the author is careful to end with a brief genealogy of the king. As previously mentioned, the book of Ruth was set during the time of the judges, between 1160 BC to 1100 BC, possibly sometime around Samson's leadership (Judges 15:20).

5. What Are the Main Themes or Keywords of the Book?

The main theme of the Bible overall is God's pursuit and redemption of His people. God's faithfulness and loyal love (*hesed*) to His people is a primary concept throughout the book of Ruth and is displayed in the relationship between Ruth and Naomi as well as in the relationship between Boaz and Ruth.

Ruth displayed the faithful love of God toward Naomi. Although a Moabite outsider, Ruth exhibited extraordinary courage and loyalty to her mother-in-law, along with an embrace of Naomi's God, Yahweh, when she left her people, her gods, and her homeland to join Naomi in her journey.

Similarly, Boaz showed God's loving kindness to Ruth and Naomi by stepping in as the *go'el*, the close relative—the kinsman-redeemer—who provided and protected vulnerable family members. He married Ruth and restored Naomi's land inheritance, shielding the two widows from poverty. Looking through the lens of the Gospels, we can see that in his role as kinsman-redeemer, Boaz is a picture of the ultimate Redeemer, Jesus. As *The Bible Knowledge Commentary* says: "Boaz is an illustration of the greater One who came from his family, the Lord Jesus Christ. Boaz acted in grace to redeem Ruth; Christ acted in grace by giving Himself as the Redeemer to provide redemption for all mankind."[2]

Though God's movement is often subtle in the book of Ruth, He ultimately is the one who redeems and restores His people. In the opening chapter, Naomi and Ruth were left destitute, grieving, and without a family. God orchestrated the events so that Naomi's lands are restored to her; Naomi and Ruth are provided for through Ruth's marriage to Boaz; and Obed, Boaz and Ruth's son, perpetuates Naomi's family line—a lineage that counts among its descendants King David and ultimately Jesus Christ.

WEEK 1

RETURNING TO GOD, RUTH 1

We have all walked through seasons of choosing our own way over God's way. It can be difficult to differentiate the voice of self over the voice of God at times, especially when it comes to trusting God with our fears and with our loved ones. But God never ceases to invite us to return to Him. Regardless how far we have strayed, His arms are open like the father to his prodigal (Luke 15:11–32). Even now—no matter your past, the burdens you carry, or your circumstances—God generously invites you to return to Him.

The book of Ruth opens with Naomi and Ruth's journey of return. Following a devastating famine in their homeland, Elimelech, Naomi, and their family sought solace in Moab, a country known for idolatry. The choice to live in a country often openly hostile to Israel and God's ways may suggest this Israelite family relied on themselves for a solution to their needs instead of seeking Yahweh's wisdom. After experiencing successive tragedies in Moab, Naomi returned home to Bethlehem. Notice the repetition of the word *return* throughout the chapter. Consider this as you spend time studying Scripture each day. Where are you in your journey with the Lord? God is always inviting you to return to Him. Let that be your invitation as you lean in and use the TEND method to hear God through His Word. Join me as we journey with this Israelite family from Israel to Moab and back again.

DAY 1

VERSES: *Ruth 1:1–5*

T. Take time to pray.

Ask the Lord to speak to you through His Word today.

TENDING TOOL: Names are important in Scripture. Most biblical names carry a meaning that gives insight into the character of the person to whom it was assigned. Consider the names of this family: *Elimelech* means "my God is King," yet Elimelech failed to live that out. *Naomi* means "pleasant" (we will see that name contrasted with the name Naomi later gave herself). *Mahlon* means "sickly," and *Chilion* means "feeble," and—reflecting the definitions of their names—the two sons had ill-health and tragically died while in Moab.

E. Examine the Scriptures.

Write out the verses from your Bible below. Pay attention to the details in these verses, such as any action taking place and repeated words or keywords used.

TENDING TOOL: In these verses, we see Elimelech and his family affected by a famine in the land where God had planted them. While they were an Israelite family given covenant promises of God, their lineage didn't shield them from the devastation in the land. To escape hardship, Elimelech led his family to sojourn to Moab, a nearby area untouched by the ravages of the famine. But then they remained there. It seems as if they sought to solve this problem in their own way, but they ended up staying longer than they anticipated.

Circle repeated words or keywords in the verses you wrote. Take note how those concepts or keywords might affect the people we are being introduced to. Put yourself in their situation.

N. Notice the lessons.

What do these verses teach about God? Remember the original audience and what the passage meant to them. In these verses, is there a sin, promise, action, command, or example to follow or not follow? Write down the lessons.

Join me as we TEND through Week 1, Day 1, together.

D. Do what it says.

Consider how you might respond to a lesson you identified. Write down your plan to carry out this lesson today. With God's grace and guidance, go do it!

DAY 2

DATE: _____   VERSES: *Ruth 1:6—9*

T. Take time to pray.

Ask the Lord to speak to you through His Word today.

E. Examine the Scriptures.

Write out the verses from your Bible below. Pay attention to the details in these verses, such as any action taking place and repeated words or keywords used.

TENDING TOOL: Remember to circle repeated words. Significantly, the same Hebrew word for *return* is repeated twelve times in this brief chapter! It is the Hebrew word *sub*, meaning "to turn, to return, to go back."[1] What a gift of grace that God never leaves us where we are and continually invites us to return to Him! Regardless of how far or for how long we have pulled away from God, we are welcomed by God when we turn back to Him.

TENDING TOOL: Naomi offered such a beautiful blessing for her daughters-in-law: "May the LORD deal kindly with you" (v. 8). This word translated *kindly* here is the Hebrew word *hesed*. *Hesed* incorporates God's covenant, steadfast love; His kindness and faithfulness; and His loyal love for His people. *The Nelson Study Bible* of the New King James Version says of this concept:

> The important idea of loyal love is evident in the book. The Hebrew word translated as *kindly* in 1:8 means "loyal love" or "covenantal love." This was a genuine love that keeps promises. When the word is used of God, it refers to God's loving faithfulness to His promises. Even though Ruth was a foreigner and was not familiar with God's law, she displayed this type of love and loyalty to her mother-in-law Naomi. She left her homeland in order to be with Naomi in a time of need. Boaz also showed the same noble quality by protecting and providing for Ruth, a widow of one of his relatives. Yet the story of Ruth ultimately illustrates how God Himself demonstrated such love. He rewarded Ruth for her loyalty to Him by giving her an honored place in the community of faith. He blessed her with a child who would become the ancestor of King David and later of the promised Messiah.[2]

Consider what Naomi's blessing reveals about God. God's covenant *hesed* is the primary theme undergirding the book—He is faithful to care for His people, and His righteous people (Ruth and Boaz) exhibit that same love.

Naomi extended a blessing over her daughters-in-law yet doubted the ability to receive the same covenant love of God for herself, as revealed in Ruth 1:13. Ask yourself if there is anything you are believing for others that you find difficult to believe for yourself. It can sometimes be easier to see God work in someone else's life than to notice His activity in our own life.

N. Notice the lessons.

What do these verses teach about God? Remember the original audience and what the passage meant to them. In these verses, is there a sin, promise, action, command, or example to follow or not follow? Write down the lessons.

D. Do what it says.

Consider how you might respond to a lesson you identified. Write down your plan to carry out this lesson today. With God's grace and guidance, go do it!

DAY 3

DATE: _____   VERSES: *Ruth 1:10–14*

T. **Take time to pray.**

Ask the Lord to speak to you through His Word today.

E. Examine the Scriptures.

Write out the verses from your Bible below. Pay attention to the details in these verses, such as any action taking place and repeated words or keywords used.

N. Notice the lessons.

What do these verses teach about God? Remember the original audience and what the passage meant to them. In these verses, is there a sin, promise, action, command, or example to follow or not follow? Write down the lessons.

TENDING TOOL: Widowed and childless, Naomi faced a bleak future, especially in a foreign country like Moab. Her love for her daughters-in-law is evident in her desire to care for them. It is important to note that widowhood and childlessness in this culture made a woman especially vulnerable. Widows were often poor and forgotten in society. Women who had buried children, like Naomi, or who were childless, like Ruth, were viewed as lacking value and had no one to care for them in their old age. These women "lacked the economic, legal and physical protection a man provided in that society."[3] Naomi had nothing to offer her daughters-in-law. Surely in her deep grief, she felt empty. Sometimes in our emptiness, we can feel like God is against us, and pushing others away only perpetuates that emptiness.

D. Do what it says.

Consider how you might respond to a lesson you identified. Write down your plan to carry out this lesson today. With God's grace and guidance, go do it!

DAY 4

DATE:_____ VERSES: *Ruth 1:15–18*

T. Take time to pray.

Ask the Lord to speak to you through His Word today.

E. Examine the Scriptures.

Write out the verses from your Bible below. Pay attention to the details in these verses, such as any action taking place and repeated words or keywords used.

TENDING TOOL: In these verses, be sure to pay attention to any keywords and repeated phrases. What is happening in these verses? How would you summarize these verses in your own words? Reread the text slowly and listen for the Holy Spirit as He highlights what is happening here. These may be familiar verses to many, but in context, they are referring to Ruth's commitment to the covenant-keeping God Naomi worshiped. She used covenant language to link herself to Naomi, her God, and the unknown future ahead. Come what may, Ruth was physically clinging to Naomi (v. 14) and spiritually clinging to Yahweh, the God of Israel. Her faith was dictating her words here and thus her actions that follow.

This is the first time we see Ruth speak, and it is with words of faith and commitment to Naomi and to her God. It can be so hard to take a step of faith when those around us are making different choices. But Ruth stood her ground. For examples of covenant-type language expressed elsewhere in the Bible, see Genesis 17:7–8 and Exodus 6:7.

What lesson begins to formulate for you as you read these verses? Is there an example you can follow here? Is there a verse or passage that you cling to in hard seasons? Take a moment to prayerfully write that down.

N. Notice the lessons.

What do these verses teach about God? Remember the original audience and what the passage meant to them. In these verses, is there a sin, promise, action, command, or example to follow or not follow? Write down the lessons.

D. Do what it says.

Consider how you might respond to a lesson you identified. Write down your plan to carry out this lesson today. With God's grace and guidance, go do it!

DAY 5

DATE:_____   VERSES: *Ruth 1:19–22*

T. Take time to pray.

Ask the Lord to speak to you through His Word today.

E. Examine the Scriptures.

Write out the verses from your Bible below. Pay attention to the details in these verses, such as any action taking place and repeated words or keywords used.

TENDING TOOL: Naomi's declared name change here is interesting. She requested that her community call her *Mara*, meaning "bitter," rather than *Naomi*, meaning "pleasant." Naomi certainly faced a seemingly hopeless situation, but she knew the truth of God's sovereignty. She had previously acknowledged Him as both "Yahweh" (v. 8, "LORD" in the ESV), which is the name used for the personal, covenant-keeping God of Israel, and "Almighty" (v. 21), yet she took on the name, and response of, Bitterness.

The writer of Hebrews warns us against bitterness (Hebrews 12:15). When we fail to see the grace of God, we are in danger of exhibiting bitterness.

N. Notice the lessons.

What do these verses teach about God? Remember the original audience and what the passage meant to them. In these verses, is there a sin, promise, action, command, or example to follow or not follow? Write down the lessons.

TENDING TOOL: As the chapter closes, the women enter Bethlehem, meaning "house of bread." Naomi and Ruth arrive in town at the beginning of the barley season, late spring, mid-April. Imagine the barley blowing in the spring breeze around them as they come near the town that Naomi had left over a decade before and that had been ravaged by famine. Now she has returned with a childless daughter-in-law and a cloak of grief and bitterness. Like Naomi, we may find ourselves in circumstances that have broken us by loss or trials. When we turn to God, He invites us to bring that pain to Him as He covers us with grace in the most unexpected ways. What do you need to bring to God in prayer today?

D. Do what it says.

Consider how you might respond to a lesson you identified. Write down your plan to carry out this lesson today. With God's grace and guidance, go do it!

DAY 6

SELAH[4] REFLECTION

Pause and reflect on lessons God has been teaching you this week. What themes highlighted in this past week do you need to bring to the Lord? Or what invitations in the biblical text do you wish to respond to? Journal your reflection below and share how you will respond, or are responding, to this week of lessons.

WEEK 2

LEARNING TO STAY, RUTH 2

When things get complicated or difficult—whether the situation involves a job, a relationship, or even a calling—my first impulse is to run. Who wants to remain when the opportunity to escape presents itself? Staying, or drawing near in the unknown, can be scary. Yet here in the second chapter of Ruth, we see that Ruth was invited to remain in her circumstances: to stay in Boaz's field to work (v. 8), to come and take refuge under the Lord's wings (v. 12), and to sit at Boaz's table (v. 14). Ruth was a woman who stayed and found safety and security in the God of Israel, even in the hardships of her life of gleaning and caring for Naomi. She never ran from her commitment, no matter the cost. Thus, she found grace in unexpected places.

The key theme of learning to stay and remain where God has called us is woven through Ruth 2. Where in our lives might God be inviting us to *stay*, *remain*, or *go back to*? Sometimes we pray for an escape when God's best might be in staying close. This absolutely *does not* mean staying in an abusive situation of any sort in a job or relationship. But we might be too quick to leave the very place God has a mind to redeem if we fail to pray and ask for His guidance. Let's lean into the faithfulness and perseverance Ruth displayed and ask God for clarity in our own circumstances.

DAY 1

DATE: _____   VERSES: *Ruth 2:1–4*

T. **Take time to pray.**

Ask the Lord to speak to you through His Word today.

E. Examine the Scriptures.

Write out the verses from your Bible below. Pay attention to the details in these verses, such as any action taking place and repeated words or keywords used.

TENDING TOOL: As the second chapter of Ruth opens, the reader is offered a bit of context. In these verses, pay attention to the description given of Boaz, as well as the unseen hand of God in directing Ruth's and Naomi's circumstances.

In the *Joseph Benson's Commentary on the Old and New Testaments* we read, "God wisely orders small events, even those that seem altogether contingent. Many a great affair is brought about by a little turn, fortuitous as to men, but designed by God."[1]

Often in the least likely place we find a powerful work of God. Can you think of an example from your own life where, in hindsight, you have seen God at work?

N. Notice the lessons.

What do these verses teach about God? Remember the original audience and what the passage meant to them. In these verses, is there a sin, promise, action, command, or example to follow or not follow? Write down the lessons.

TENDING TOOL: Read Leviticus 19:9–10 to learn more about gleaning and gain context on what Ruth was doing and how gleaning benefited her and Naomi. *Gleaning* was the gathering of grain intentionally left in a field by the reapers: "Mosaic law required leaving this portion so that the poor and aliens might have a means of earning a living."[2]

The greeting between Boaz and his reapers in verse 4 reveals Boaz's faith. Both Boaz and his employees referred to God as "Lord," which in Hebrew is "Yahweh" or "YHWH." This is the personal name of God given to Moses for God's people in Exodus 3. But it is also the covenant name of God through which God continually extended Himself to His people. We see this illustrated in the first mention of the name Yahweh in Genesis 2, where His continual interactions with Adam demonstrate God's desire for a personal relationship with humankind. In chapter 2, Yahweh is said to have formed the man, placed him in the garden, given him instructions, and caused him to sleep so as to form the woman for the man. Then in Genesis 3, after Adam and Eve's sin, Yahweh is the one who initiated the restoration of their relationship with Him in verse 9. When God sent our perfect Redeemer, Jesus, whose name means "Yahweh saves," He initiated the restoration of our relationship.

D. Do what it says.

Consider how you might respond to a lesson you identified. Write down your plan to carry out this lesson today. With God's grace and guidance, go do it!

DAY 2

DATE: _____   VERSES: *Ruth 2:5–9*

T. Take time to pray.

Ask the Lord to speak to you through His Word today.

E. Examine the Scriptures.

Write out the verses from your Bible below. Pay attention to the details in these verses, such as any action taking place and repeated words or keywords used.

TENDING TOOL: In the book of Ruth, Ruth is repeatedly mentioned as a Moabitess or as being from Moab. Twice her origin in Moab is specified in verse 6 alone. It is important to note that Moab was a country about seventy miles outside of Bethlehem whose people were spiritually far from God. They descended from Lot and his oldest daughter who, following the destruction of Sodom and Gomorrah, had sexual relations (see Genesis 19:30–38). The child born of that incestuous union was Moab, who grew to be a pagan man whose descendants worshiped the false god Chemosh.

Ruth turned from the familiarity of Moab and the worship of Chemosh to the unknowns of Bethlehem and the worship of Yahweh. Consider when you might have had to step out of the familiar into the unknown to follow God, whether in a new season of life, new location, new job, or new relationship. How might this grow your faith?

N. Notice the lessons.

What do these verses teach about God? Remember the original audience and what the passage meant to them. In these verses, is there a sin, promise, action, command, or example to follow or not follow? Write down the lessons.

TENDING TOOL: A couple repeated words begin to appear in the opening verses of this chapter, *come* and *keep close*. As chapter 1 was sprinkled with the repetition of *return*, we see chapter 2 filled with invitations *to come*, meaning "to draw near." In your own life, ponder where you are being invited to draw near to God.

The phrase translated "keep close" in verse 8 is the same word used in Psalm 63:7–8 when the psalmist tells us he was clinging to the Lord. The word (in Hebrew, *dabaq*) means "to cling, cleave, and keep close to another." *Dabaq* is also alluded to when Ruth "clung" to Naomi in Ruth 1:14. Ruth clung to Naomi, and now Boaz has invited Ruth to do the same to his servant women, for the sake of her protection.

Ruth's clinging in verse 14 demonstrated her remarkable faithfulness to Naomi. That faithfulness was the foundation on which Boaz insisted the Moabitess cling to his servants. Later in the chapter, in verse 23, we see Ruth continue to cling to the servant women at Naomi's instruction. As you reflect on Ruth's faithfulness, take time to consider your current responsibilities, circumstances, and relationships. In what area of your life might God be inviting you into greater faithfulness?

RUTH

D. Do what it says.

Consider how you might respond to a lesson you identified. Write down your plan to carry out this lesson today. With God's grace and guidance, go do it!

DAY 3

DATE: _____   VERSES: *Ruth 2:10–13*

T. **Take time to pray.**

Ask the Lord to speak to you through His Word today.

E. Examine the Scriptures.

Write out the verses from your Bible below. Pay attention to the details in these verses, such as any action taking place and repeated words or keywords used.

N. Notice the lessons.

What do these verses teach about God? Remember the original audience and what the passage meant to them. In these verses, is there a sin, promise, action, command, or example to follow or not follow? Write down the lessons.

TENDING TOOL: It's interesting to note here that Boaz spoke to Ruth with respect, even inviting her to dine at his table in verse 14, which was an act of inclusion, of shared fellowship and trust. Boaz was going beyond the requirements of the Law in his provisions for Ruth.[3] With his own mother, Rahab, being a foreign woman who put her trust in Yahweh (see Joshua 2), certainly he could see beyond Ruth's lineage to her faithfulness and courage. In these verses, he even noticed her motives: her faithfulness to her mother-in-law and her desire to seek refuge "under the wings" of Yahweh (v. 12), the God of Israel.

Beautiful cross-references of the imagery of taking refuge under God's "wings" are found in Psalms 17:7–8; 36:7; 57:1; and 91:4. They are worth considering as you pray through these verses today, meditating on a time you have sought refuge in the Lord. What might taking refuge under His wings look like for you today?

D. Do what it says.

Consider how you might respond to a lesson you identified. Write down your plan to carry out this lesson today. With God's grace and guidance, go do it!

DAY 4

DATE: _____   VERSES: *Ruth 2:14–18*

T. Take time to pray.

Ask the Lord to speak to you through His Word today.

E. Examine the Scriptures.

Write out the verses from your Bible below. Pay attention to the details in these verses, such as any action taking place and repeated words or keywords used.

TENDING TOOL: Boaz extended another invitation to "come" (v. 14), translated here from the Hebrew *nagash*. This time it was an invitation to draw near and to eat at his table. David Camera, an Old Testament scholar, offers, "We learn in the Bible that sharing a meal together is one of the primary ways relationships are established, deepened, and enjoyed both with God and with others. Think of the covenant meal the elders of Israel enjoyed with God on Mount Sinai."[4] The significance of sharing a meal together is worth considering as we see the unfolding of this narrative.

N. Notice the lessons.

What do these verses teach about God? Remember the original audience and what the passage meant to them. In these verses, is there a sin, promise, action, command, or example to follow or not follow? Write down the lessons.

TENDING TOOL: Many of the people God spotlights in the Bible are meant to highlight characteristics of God Himself. Consider how Boaz and Ruth showcase God's attributes throughout this book. Continue to notice Boaz's demeanor and interactions with Ruth, a foreign widow in Bethlehem.

Also pay attention to how Ruth demonstrates characteristics of God's kindness and mercy as the caregiver of her widowed mother-in-law. Even though a widow herself, Ruth does not have self-focused motives but rather compassion on the one God has entrusted her to care for. The *Holman Illustrated Bible Dictionary* shares about God's perspective on the treatment of widows: "Special consideration for widows is first mentioned in Exodus 22:22. Since God has compassion on widows, we should do the same. When a nation and its leaders do so, they are promised a blessing."[5] Cross-references to consider: Deuteronomy 14:29; Psalms 68:5; 146:9; Jeremiah 7:5–7; 1 Timothy 5:3; James 1:27.

D. Do what it says.

Consider how you might respond to a lesson you identified. Write down your plan to carry out this lesson today. With God's grace and guidance, go do it!

DAY 5

DATE: _____   VERSES: *Ruth 2:19–23*

T. Take time to pray.

Ask the Lord to speak to you through His Word today.

E. Examine the Scriptures.

Write out the verses from your Bible below. Pay attention to the details in these verses, such as any action taking place and repeated words or keywords used.

TENDING TOOL: A keyword in the book of Ruth we have previously looked at is stated again in verse 20, translated "kindness" (in Hebrew, *hesed*). *Hesed* is used about 250 times in the Old Testament. The closest English definitions of the word include "kindness," "steadfast love," "graciousness," "mercy," "goodness," and "faithfulness." None of these words adequately translate the meaning of this beautiful, descriptive word most often used to define the unmatchable character of God. *Hesed* is the motive of God for nearly everything He does. Psalm 136 illustrates this through the repetition of the word in each of the psalm's twenty-six verses, beginning with the opening verse: "Give thanks to the LORD, for he is good, for his steadfast love [*hesed*] endures forever."

Another key phrase, *keep close*, which we saw in Ruth 2:8–10, is repeated again here in verse 23. Ruth kept close to the women and labored with the encouragement of Naomi, knowing Yahweh was her refuge (Ruth 2:12).

N. Notice the lessons.

What do these verses teach about God? Remember the original audience and what the passage meant to them. In these verses, is there a sin, promise, action, command, or example to follow or not follow? Write down the lessons.

TENDING TOOL: Naomi advised that Ruth keep close to Boaz's field. She pointed out that he is a kinsman-redeemer—a key concept for us to define. The kinsman-redeemer was the next of kin who would secure the freedom or protection for the family. The act of redemption could involve marriage, land purchase, and inheritance laws.

In the ancient Near East, the kinsman-redeemer had to be willing to make a large sacrifice since he could be jeopardizing the inheritance for his children, potentially shrinking the value of his estate for his descendants.[6] The redeemer's role was voluntary. When a family member accepted the kinsman-redeemer's offer, she would enter into relationship with her kinsman-redeemer, as we will see with Ruth and Boaz, and be provided for. The Hebrew word translated "redeemer" in Ruth is *go'el*. The same word is used of God Himself in Isaiah 60:16. Looking through the lens of the Gospels, we see the word offers us a picture of our ultimate Redeemer, Jesus (1 Peter 1:18–19). He is the one who would redeem fully by laying down His own life willingly to offer eternal life to every one of us who would surrender to Him. Consider meditating on some of the beautiful cross-references: Romans 8:16–17; Ephesians 1:11; Colossians 1:12; and 1 Peter 1:3–4.

D. Do what it says.

Consider how you might respond to a lesson you identified. Write down your plan to carry out this lesson today. With God's grace and guidance, go do it!

DAY 6

SELAH REFLECTION

Pause and reflect on lessons God has been teaching you this week. What themes highlighted in this past week do you need to bring to the Lord? Or what invitations in the biblical text do you wish to respond to? Journal your reflection below and share how you will respond, or are responding, to this week of lessons.

WEEK 3

AN ACTIVE PURSUIT OF REST, RUTH 3

Naomi desired that Ruth find rest in the home of a husband. In the ancient Near East, this would mean provision, protection, and redemption for her dear daughter-in-law who, as a widow, was especially vulnerable. Ruth was not passive in seeking this rest.

In Hebrews 4, the author speaks of the rest that God offers His people through salvation in Jesus only, not through our works. Yet in Hebrews 4:9–11, we see a rest we are to strive toward. Verse 11 says, "Let us therefore strive to enter that rest, so that no one may fall by the same sort of disobedience." The rest that God offers is eternal and based fully on the work of Christ. His people are invited to strive toward growing in intimacy with Him in response to His free offer.

The active pursuit of rest that we find Ruth engaging in as she seeks her kinsman-redeemer in Boaz can—when viewed through the metanarrative of Scripture—become a beautiful illustration of our own pursuit of growing in our relationship with Christ, our kinsman-redeemer. Bible scholar Warren Wiersbe says, "[This chapter] is also the picture of Christ's relationship to those who trust Him and belong to Him. In the steps Ruth takes recorded in this chapter, we see the steps God's people must take if they want to enter into a deeper relationship with the Lord. Like Ruth, we must not be satisfied merely with living on leftovers (2:2), or even receiving gifts (2:14, 16). We must want Him alone, for when we have Him, we also have all that He owns. It's not the gifts that we seek, but the Giver."[1] As we look at the passage through the lens of the Gospels, contemplate the Giver's heart toward you.

DAY 1

DATE: _____   VERSES: *Ruth 3:1–5*

T. Take time to pray.

Ask the Lord to speak to you through His Word today.

TENDING TOOL: Chapter 3 opens with Naomi's desire for Ruth to find *rest* in the home of a husband (v. 1). This is from the Hebrew word transliterated *manoach*, a noun meaning "a resting place," "a place of security." It points to a location where something settles down and remains. It can also mean "the cessation of work to refresh oneself." For the New Testament believer, Jesus is our resting place.

Naomi shared with Ruth how she must prepare to enter this rest—by washing and anointing herself and putting on her best attire. God is the one who prepares us for the rest we find in Him. Warren Wiersbe points out that we come to Jesus washed through repentance (2 Corinthians 7:1; Psalm 51:2, 7), and that He anoints us by His Spirit (1 John 2:20) with the garments of salvation (Isaiah 61:10).[2]

As you draw near to God today, lean in through the repentance of sin, grateful for the gift of forgiveness every believer is offered in Jesus. Thank Him for the anointing of His Spirit and the garments of salvation promised to every believer.

E. Examine the Scriptures.

Write out the verses from your Bible below. Pay attention to the details in these verses, such as any action taking place and repeated words or keywords used.

TENDING TOOL: Just as Naomi shared with Ruth the practical steps of approaching Boaz, we can consider practical steps to approaching Christ through His Word. As you consider what these verses teach about God, ask God to show you how you might lean in to knowing and loving Him in response to His love for you. Often leaning in simply means being willing to respond in obedience to what God reveals to us. Ruth promised to obey Naomi's direction. She not only listened to Naomi but, in obeying, she revealed her trust in Naomi. James 1:22 challenges us to be not only hearers of the Word but doers of the Word. How might you walk in obedience today to what God is revealing to you?

N. Notice the lessons.

What do these verses teach about God? Remember the original audience and what the passage meant to them. In these verses, is there a sin, promise, action, command, or example to follow or not follow? Write down the lessons.

D. Do what it says.

Consider how you might respond to a lesson you identified. Write down your plan to carry out this lesson today. With God's grace and guidance, go do it!

DAY 2

DATE: _____   VERSES: *Ruth 3:6–9*

T. Take time to pray.

Ask the Lord to speak to you through His Word today.

E. Examine the Scriptures.

Write out the verses from your Bible below. Pay attention to the details in these verses, such as any action taking place and repeated words or keywords used.

TENDING TOOL: There is such an interesting repetition found in Ruth's appeal to Boaz in verse 9: "Spread your *wings* over your servant, for you are a redeemer" (emphasis added). Ruth echoed the wording of Boaz's blessing over her in Ruth 2:12. She also acknowledged his relation to her as a redeemer. Her request is bold and seemingly confident in the fulfillment of the redemption she sought. How can you pray boldly and confidently in the promise of your own redemption in Jesus?

N. Notice the lessons.

What do these verses teach about God? Remember the original audience and what the passage meant to them. In these verses, is there a sin, promise, action, command, or example to follow or not follow? Write down the lessons.

TENDING TOOL: Just as Boaz had noted that Ruth had found refuge under the wings of Yahweh (2:12), in verse 9 she asked that Boaz "spread [his wings]" over her by becoming her husband. The word for "wings" can also mean "corners of a garment." The New International Version translates Ruth's words as "Spread the corner of your garment over me." According to Warren Wiersbe, "To spread one's mantle over a person meant to claim that person for yourself (Ezekiel 16:8, 1 Kings 19:19), particularly in marriage."[3]

Consider how in your current season you might need to find refuge under the cover of your Redeemer, Jesus. How can you respond today to the truth that He is your refuge?

D. Do what it says.

Consider how you might respond to a lesson you identified. Write down your plan to carry out this lesson today. With God's grace and guidance, go do it!

DAY 3

DATE:_____   VERSES: *Ruth 3:10–13*

T. Take time to pray.

Ask the Lord to speak to you through His Word today.

E. Examine the Scriptures.

Write out the verses from your Bible below. Pay attention to the details in these verses, such as any action taking place and repeated words or keywords used.

TENDING TOOL: When you examine the Scripture passage by slowing down and paying attention to the details, it is important to remember the context by identifying the pronouns mentioned. When *he/she* or *I* is used in a verse, it makes a difference to notice who the text is referring to based on the previous verses and the context of the chapter at large. This gives clarity about what is happening in the scene and who is talking to whom.

N. Notice the lessons.

What do these verses teach about God? Remember the original audience and what the passage meant to them. In these verses, is there a sin, promise, action, command, or example to follow or not follow? Write down the lessons.

TENDING TOOL: Consider two important words found in verses 10 through 13. One is the compliment Boaz offered Ruth in verse 11. The word *chayil*—translated "worthy" in the English Standard Version—is the same word praising the Proverbs 31 woman in Proverbs 31:10. *Chayil* is a military word. It can mean "strength," "efficiency," "wealth," and "army." With a powerful meaning in Scripture, *chayil* describes men like Gideon (Judges 6:12) and Boaz (Ruth 2:1), but here we find Boaz using it to describe Ruth. This speaks to Ruth's strength of character.

Second, the Hebrew word *go'el*, translated "redeemer," one of our keywords, is mentioned six times in these verses. *Go'el* denotes being "bought back by payment." It refers to a personal relationship. What does this word's meaning tell you about the role of—and our relationship with—our Redeemer?

D. Do what it says.

Consider how you might respond to a lesson you identified. Write down your plan to carry out this lesson today. With God's grace and guidance, go do it!

DAY 4

DATE: _____   VERSES: *Ruth 3:14—15*

T. Take time to pray.

Ask the Lord to speak to you through His Word today.

TENDING TOOL: As this interaction between Ruth and Boaz on the threshing floor unfolds, we see the heart of Boaz with greater clarity as well as his faith in Yahweh.

Boaz was a man of wealth and property, but that would not automatically have made him generous. Yet he received Ruth with generosity. He measured out six measures of barley for Ruth to share with Naomi. Likely sixty to eighty pounds of grain, this amount was twice what Ruth would have gleaned by herself. What a display of God's abundance!

In Warren Wiersbe's comments on verses 14 through 15, he points out: "In the responses of Boaz to Ruth, we see how the Lord responds to us when we seek to have a deeper fellowship with Him."[4]

E. Examine the Scriptures.

Write out the verses from your Bible below. Pay attention to the details in these verses, such as any action taking place and repeated words or keywords used.

N. Notice the lessons.

What do these verses teach about God? Remember the original audience and what the passage meant to them. In these verses, is there a sin, promise, action, command, or example to follow or not follow? Write down the lessons.

D. Do what it says.

Consider how you might respond to a lesson you identified. Write down your plan to carry out this lesson today. With God's grace and guidance, go do it!

DAY 5

DATE: _____   VERSES: *Ruth 3:16–18*

T. Take time to pray.

Ask the Lord to speak to you through His Word today.

TENDING TOOL: Ruth returned with an abundance of grain to share with Naomi as confirmation of the promise to come (v. 18). Boaz had expressed his willingness to see to it that Ruth was redeemed, whether by himself or another relative. While Ruth had not come asking for the physical need of food to be met, he provided it anyway. This was priceless for her and her widowed mother-in-law in a society where widowhood left a woman in a desperate, impoverished state. Women whose husbands had died were left without provision, protection, or a means to get either. Boaz's actions toward Naomi and Ruth reflect God's heart toward the destitute. The Old Testament repeatedly identifies three vulnerable groups whom God called His people to care for: widows, orphans, and immigrants (see Deuteronomy 10:18). The *righteous* (in Hebrew, *tsaddikim*)—such as Boaz—were upright and were concerned with those often-oppressed groups.

Similarly, in the New Testament, we read of God's call to the Christian community to support widows and orphans: "Religion that God our Father accepts as pure and faultless is this: to look after orphans and widows in their distress" (James 1:27). How might you see the vulnerable and oppressed as God does and respond with grace and abundance today?

E. Examine the Scriptures.

Write out the verses from your Bible below. Pay attention to the details in these verses, such as any action taking place and repeated words or keywords used.

TENDING TOOL: As we close chapter 3, we see Naomi now experiencing fullness rather than emptiness, physically and likely spiritually too. If you are walking through an empty season today, how can you lean into the Lord while holding space for grief or loss? Is there a truth you can meditate on? Sometimes remembering the character of God and giving thanks can renew our minds and bring healing in a difficult season. Consider making a list of the gifts God has provided you physically, emotionally, and spiritually in the last week. Praising God often helps us remember He is our Shepherd, and that we have all we need (Psalm 23:1).

N. Notice the lessons.

What do these verses teach about God? Remember the original audience and what the passage meant to them. In these verses, is there a sin, promise, action, command, or example to follow or not follow? Write down the lessons.

D. Do what it says.

Consider how you might respond to a lesson you identified. Write down your plan to carry out this lesson today. With God's grace and guidance, go do it!

DAY 6

SELAH REFLECTION

Pause and reflect on lessons God has been teaching you this week. What themes highlighted in this past week do you need to bring to the Lord? Or what invitations in the biblical text do you wish to respond to? Journal your reflection below and share how you will respond, or are responding, to this week of lessons.

WEEK 4

REDEMPTION, RUTH 4

Redemption is central to the heart of God. Through all of Scripture, we see God redeem His broken, sinful people and reconcile them to Himself. In this last portion of Ruth, we see the beautiful conclusion of Ruth's redemption, which paved the way for the redemption of her lineage as well as all who would place their faith in Jesus.

We are all lost and in need of redemption. God sent His Son, Jesus, to redeem the lost by paying the price with His own life. Looking through the lens of the Gospels, we can see Boaz as a picture of the Redeemer throughout the book of Ruth. Now we see it in greater color as we reach the finale. Consider the lessons God revealed to you through the week and the study. Ask God where He might be redeeming an area of your life in this season as He draws you near and invites you to return to Him. I then invite you to trace the line of Ruth into the New Testament by reading Matthew 1:5–6, then on to the end of Matthew 1, where we see not only those in the lineage of Christ but the birth of the One who is *Emmanuel*, God with us. The theme of redemption is stretched from our Moabitess to you and the family line after you, an unexpected grace indeed. Let's lean in and ask God to continue to tend these truths into our hearts and lives long after we have closed the book of Ruth.

DAY 1

DATE: _____   VERSES: *Ruth 4:1–4*

T.   Take time to pray.

Ask the Lord to speak to you through His Word today.

E. Examine the Scriptures.

Write out the verses from your Bible below. Pay attention to the details in these verses, such as any action taking place and repeated words or keywords used.

TENDING TOOL: Do you see the providence of God demonstrated in these verses as you saw earlier in Ruth 2:3–4? Though God is not implicitly mentioned here, the narrator gives us the sense of God's presence and handiwork in the phrasing "Behold, the redeemer, of whom Boaz had spoken, came by" (v. 1). Paying attention to God's hand and activity in Scripture can often help us see His work and movement in our lives more clearly.

N. Notice the lessons.

What do these verses teach about God? Remember the original audience and what the passage meant to them. In these verses, is there a sin, promise, action, command, or example to follow or not follow? Write down the lessons.

TENDING TOOL: The English Standard Version designates the unknown redeemer as "friend" (v. 1), but the Hebrew wording is less respectful. The original translation highlights the namelessness and obscurity of the man who refused to lay aside his comforts for the good of another. In Hebrew the man is referred to with an idiom equivalent to "Mr. So-and-So." Mr. So-and-So missed out on being a part of the story of redemption because he was self-focused instead of trusting God's design.

On the other hand, we see Boaz's willingness to take on the financial and providential care of Naomi and Ruth. He also married Ruth with the intent of fathering her firstborn for Elimelech's line rather than his own. Because of Boaz's sacrificial willingness, he was used by God in a story far greater than he could have imagined.

God could have used anyone or no one. Boaz was the vessel who trusted in His guidance. How can you live with a willingness to follow Jesus more than anything or anyone else?

D. Do what it says.

Consider how you might respond to a lesson you identified. Write down your plan to carry out this lesson today. With God's grace and guidance, go do it!

DAY 2

DATE: _____   VERSES: *Ruth 4:5–8*

T. Take time to pray.

Ask the Lord to speak to you through His Word today.

E. Examine the Scriptures.

Write out the verses from your Bible below. Pay attention to the details in these verses, such as any action taking place and repeated words or keywords used.

TENDING TOOL: After writing out verses 5 through 8 from your Bible, circle the repeated words you see, specifically in the first kinsman-redeemer's response to Boaz. What does this tell you about his motives and character? And how do they differ from the heart of God toward the widow or immigrant, as we have previously seen?

N. Notice the lessons.

What do these verses teach about God? Remember the original audience and what the passage meant to them. In these verses, is there a sin, promise, action, command, or example to follow or not follow? Write down the lessons.

TENDING TOOL: Just like the first kinsman-redeemer, we have a limited perspective. Take a glimpse of the ancestors in Christ's lineage by reading Matthew 1:1–17. We see this man was being offered the opportunity to be part of the line of Jesus. Though he didn't know that at the time, God did. It's interesting to consider what, at times, might seem costly from our perspective offers abundant grace from God's perspective.

Customs found in Scripture can lose meaning for us in the Western world. This is when it can be helpful to dig a bit to gain perspective. *Ellicott's Commentary for English Readers* offers one perspective about this unique custom: "**Plucked off his shoe**—the idea of this act is that the man resigns the right of walking on the land as master, in favor of him whom he gives the shoe."[1] *The IVP Bible Background Commentary* adds: "Since they walked off the land in sandals, the sandals became the movable title to that land."[2]

D. Do what it says.

Consider how you might respond to a lesson you identified. Write down your plan to carry out this lesson today. With God's grace and guidance, go do it!

DAY 3

VERSES: *Ruth 4:9–12*

T. Take time to pray.

Ask the Lord to speak to you through His Word today.

TENDING TOOL: After writing down Ruth 4:9–12, consider the Israelite ancestors mentioned in verses 11 and 12. Their complicated stories highlight the grace of our Redeemer. In Genesis 29–35, we read of Jacob's two wives: sisters Leah and Rachel. Rachel was loved by Jacob, but Leah wasn't, as Jacob was tricked into marrying her first. But through these sisters came the children who would become the twelve tribes of Israel.

Also mentioned in this blessing are Tamar and Judah (Jacob's son), whose sad story is found in Genesis 38. Tamar disguised herself as a prostitute; slept with her father-in-law, Judah; and conceived twins through Judah after he unjustly denied her the right of bearing a child through his family line. Perez, mentioned in Ruth 4:12, is one of their sons. Yet in all the dysfunction, this family line founded Israel—a reflection of the unexpected grace of God. And the witnesses to Ruth and Boaz's marriage invoked this family tree's memory in their blessings over the new couple (vv. 11–12).

The prayers of those witnesses for favor and blessing over Boaz and Ruth's offspring would be answered long after their lifetimes, when Jesus the Messiah would come through this line.

E. Examine the Scriptures.

Write out the verses from your Bible below. Pay attention to the details in these verses, such as any action taking place and repeated words or keywords used.

TENDING TOOL: As we see in the illustration of this stingy kinsman-redeemer, redemption required sacrifice. Contrasted to the first redeemer, Boaz had "undertaken the total care of Naomi and the obligation to support her in life and provide for her in death." The *IVP Bible Background Commentary* continues, "By acquiring Ruth, he has obligated himself to give her the opportunity to bear children, the first of whom would then be the heir of Elimelech and his sons."[3]

Consider the truths of 1 Corinthians 6:19–20 and the cost of God's love for you.

N. Notice the lessons.

What do these verses teach about God? Remember the original audience and what the passage meant to them. In these verses, is there a sin, promise, action, command, or example to follow or not follow? Write down the lessons.

D. Do what it says.

Consider how you might respond to a lesson you identified. Write down your plan to carry out this lesson today. With God's grace and guidance, go do it!

DAY 4

DATE:_____   VERSES: *Ruth 4:13–17*

T. **Take time to pray.**

Ask the Lord to speak to you through His Word today.

E. Examine the Scriptures.

Write out the verses from your Bible below. Pay attention to the details in these verses, such as any action taking place and repeated words or keywords used.

TENDING TOOL: The woman who had been childless for ten years while married to her first husband in Moab now conceived a son (v. 13). Sometimes the very thing we pray for and do not get becomes the arrow that points out the faithfulness of God we would not have seen any other way.

N. Notice the lessons.

What do these verses teach about God? Remember the original audience and what the passage meant to them. In these verses, is there a sin, promise, action, command, or example to follow or not follow? Write down the lessons.

TENDING TOOL: In Ruth 4:14–15 and 17, notice what the women of the town were now saying to Naomi compared to their initial interaction with her in Ruth 1:19–21.

While Naomi may have legally adopted Ruth's son, the naming of Obed as Naomi's more likely reflects the fact that this child represented the redeemed line of Elimelech: Because of Boaz's action as the *go'el*, Boaz and Ruth's firstborn son would be the successor of Naomi's late husband.[4] Obed is called a "restorer of life" for Naomi (v. 15). The word translated *restorer* in the English Standard Version is the same Hebrew phrase repeatedly mentioned in chapter 1—*return*. Having returned to Bethlehem empty, Naomi now was full of hope and joy as she held the child Obed and experienced all God had redeemed in her life. The pain of her past losses was not forgotten, but God breathed a fresh hope over Naomi. Yet the hope did not come as Naomi expected.

God invites us to return and to be restored as well (consider Psalm 23:3). His redemption and blessings may not manifest themselves in ways we expect, but we can trust in the promise of His restoration. How have you seen God invite you to fresh hope?

D. Do what it says.

Consider how you might respond to a lesson you identified. Write down your plan to carry out this lesson today. With God's grace and guidance, go do it!

DAY 5

DATE: _____   VERSES: *Ruth 4:18–22*

T. Take time to pray.

Ask the Lord to speak to you through His Word today.

TENDING TOOL: The epilogue of Ruth (vv. 18–22) offers hope. This brief genealogy reveals the future of Boaz and Ruth's line, which is the lineage of King David. Such a revelation would have been meaningful to the original hearers and readers. But as New Testament believers, we can see the significance of this family line to an even greater extent as we trace it through the pen of the apostle Matthew in Matthew 1:1–17. The book of Ruth opens with emptiness, poverty, and such hopelessness, yet the book concludes with fullness, provision, and a forward-looking hope of eternal healing in the ultimate Redeemer.

Through broken people entangled in sin, God still works, redeems, heals, and draws people to Himself. What brokenness in your family line seems as if it's beyond the scope of God's restoration and healing? The book of Ruth stands as an objection to our limited perspective.

E. Examine the Scriptures.

Write out the verses from your Bible below. Pay attention to the details in these verses, such as any action taking place and repeated words or keywords used.

N. Notice the lessons.

What do these verses teach about God? Remember the original audience and what the passage meant to them. In these verses, is there a sin, promise, action, command, or example to follow or not follow? Write down the lessons.

RUTH

D. Do what it says.

Consider how you might respond to a lesson you identified. Write down your plan to carry out this lesson today. With God's grace and guidance, go do it!

DAY 6

A s you conclude the book of Ruth, pause and reflect on the lessons God has been teaching you. What stood out to you about the character of God? Are you being called to pray about specific themes or to respond to any invitations in the text? What main takeaway has God been highlighting for you throughout this study? Journal your reflection and response to what God has been teaching you.

A CLOSING THOUGHT

As we close out this journey through the book of Ruth using the TEND method, I want to encourage you to continue to tend your soul as a gardener tends her garden. We will only ever be as healthy as our soul. As the apostle John wrote to the church, "Beloved, I pray that all may go well with you and that you may be in good health, as it goes well with your soul" (3 John 2).

May the fruit God bears in and through you as a result of the time you have spent in His Word these last few weeks point many people to our good and gracious heavenly Father. Thank you for journeying with me through the book of Ruth. I look forward to meeting you again in the Word.

Keep tending your soul,

Mariel

Interested in facilitating a TEND group? Check out my Leader's Guide!

APPENDIX A

Which Bible Translation Should I Use?

The English language is blessed with *many* translations of the Bible. Some languages have only one translation (or even none!). But your grandmother's dusty King James Bible—with its stilted, difficult language—might not be the best translation for you. Yet your child or grandchild's preschool picture Bible won't work either.

How do you find the right Bible for you? And is there a "right" translation?

First, rather than getting frustrated with the plurality of options, let's praise God for the men and women who went before us, enabling much of the Western world to have Bibles in their language. Over the centuries, translations have been sharpened and tweaked in an effort to best translate languages that are very different from ours.

When considering translations, think of them on a spectrum. No one translation has the edge over another. The Bible was written in

Hebrew, Aramaic, and Greek—not in English—so every single English translation is an attempt at taking the God-breathed words and idioms of one language and expressing them in another.

Before we look at a few translations, know that it is best to use multiple translations. For example, I primarily use one version for my time with the Lord and for study. But I also routinely access other translations on Bible Hub to gain insight on the original languages of the Bible. Various translators have different goals in translating and, as a result, may translate phrases differently. This can be valuable insight for Bible study.

Translations are categorized as literal, dynamic, or paraphrastic. When determining the best versions for Bible study, you may find it helpful to choose one from each category since their translators have a different objective for their particular translation.

Literal translations are word-for-word styles that boast of being the closest to the original text. But the reality is that for the versions to make sense in English, scholars' interpretations influence even these translations. These Bible versions attempt to translate words with only small changes to sentence structure; thus, they can contain unnatural rhythms or awkward wording.

Dynamic translations are considered thought-for-thought translations. The translators do more of the work by translating a concept from the ancient language into a similar idea in English. Their objective is to find a balance between readability and the original wording. Thus, these translations interpret words and sentence structure as they help with clarity.

Finally, **paraphrastic translations** are the scholars' paraphrase of the original words and the meaning behind them. For paraphrases, the objective is readability. The Bible scholars who create paraphrastic translations are offering fully translated passages and modernized idioms and thoughts.

Examples of each style of translation are listed below. Much on translations, and the differences between them, can be found through an online search or by calling a Christian bookstore. Sources can place the translations in various categories, and even the quality of different editions of the same translation can be debated. Be careful not to get tangled up in the details of these highly contested topics! Just choose a translation that you understand and will use, because the best translation is a used translation.

Literal

English Standard Version (ESV). A revision of the Revised Standard Version (RSV), the English Standard Version features a tenth-grade reading level. It is quickly becoming one of the most used English translations in America.

King James Version (KJV). One of the most popular versions of the Bible since its first publication in 1611, the King James Version is written in Early Modern English, which can make it a more difficult translation for most people to understand. It has an upper–high-school reading level.

New American Standard Bible (NASB). Considered the most literal translation by many, the New American Standard Bible is written at an upper–high-school level. This translation has been revised multiple times under the same name with different copyright years.

New King James Version (NKJV). A revision of the King James Version, the New King James Version—which has a seventh-grade reading level—uses more modern wording than the King James Version and is thus easier to understand.

Dynamic

Christian Standard Bible (CSB). This version combines word-for-word with thought-for thought translation and is at a seventh-grade reading level. It is a revision of the Holman Christian Standard Bible.

New International Version (NIV). This translation is often used for translating the Bible into other languages, such as Spanish. The New International Version is considered to have a seventh-grade reading level.

New Living Translation (NLT). With an elementary reading level, this version is considered highly readable. The translators have done much of the interpreting work for us.

Paraphrastic

The Message (MSG). Offering modernized wording, this is a paraphrase by linguistics scholar Eugene Peterson, written at an elementary reading level. Peterson created The Message with the aim of offering his congregation an easy-to-understand version of the Bible.

The Living Bible (TLB). Popular in the 1970s and 1980s, this paraphrase is written at an elementary reading level. In the late 1980s, its creator, Kenneth N. Taylor, president of Christian publisher Tyndale House, invited nearly 100 ancient language scholars to revise the text—which led to the making of the New Living Translation, a dynamic translation.

APPENDIX B

Resources for Further Study

Choosing and utilizing dependable resources is important in Bible study. The commentaries, dictionaries, and encyclopedias that we choose can lead us astray if they are not of solid doctrine. Below are a few of the reliable resources I have found helpful in my own study. As you gather your own resources, you might consider asking a pastor, trusted Christian leader, or teacher for other good resources.

Keywords

The Bible was originally written in ancient Greek, Aramaic, and Hebrew. To gain a clearer understanding of a repeated word, or a common word, or just a word or phrase that stands out to you, it can be helpful to return to these original languages. Thankfully, in our digital age, you do not have to be a linguistics scholar to gain a general understanding of the words. Reliable online resources created by linguistic scholars can help guide us. Below are some resources I use.

- Bible Gateway
- Bible Hub

- Blue Letter Bible
- Logos Bible Software

I find that uncovering and plugging the original definition of a Bible word back into a verse can clarify the verse's meaning. Using multiple translations can also serve this purpose. For example, when a passage feels repetitive in a more formal translation, I sometimes read a dynamic or paraphrastic translation to better understand the context.

Cross-References

The best way to interpret the Bible is with the Bible. Even though around forty different men were used to pen the words of the Bible, God Himself is the author of it all. And just as a book written by a human is best explained by the author, so it is with the Bible. The best way to let Scripture explain Scripture is with cross-references.

Some Bibles provide cross-references. These cross-references are not inspired by God, so if another reference comes to mind, it is likely just as solid as what is offered on the page.

A cross-reference is simply another verse that contains the same word or idea as the one you are studying. For example, Jeremiah 29:11; Isaiah 55:8–12; and Psalm 33:11 are cross-references that refer to the thoughts or plans of the Lord.

Cross-references are also places where a previously mentioned passage is being quoted; for example, the New Testament often refers to Old Testament passages. We see this in Hebrews chapter 1 where the author is pointing to several Old Testament verses in succession. In Hebrews 1:5, he is quoting Psalm 2:7; 2 Samuel 7:14; and 1 Chronicles 17:13. To better understand what the author of Hebrews is saying to the original audience, it is wise to return to the Old Testament cross-references and study the context of those passages.

In addition to being included in many references and study Bibles, cross-references are also offered by the following digital resources:

- Bible Gateway

- Bible Hub
- Blue Letter Bible
- Logos Bible Software

Commentaries

Commentaries contain comments from someone on a verse, passage, or book of the Bible. Reliable commentaries were written by scholars and theologians who have spent years studying the nuances of a book of the Bible and offer great insight and interpretation. Here are two important tips when using commentaries:

- *Don't begin with them.* Let the Spirit of God speak to you through the Word of God as you TEND through a verse or passage. Journal or pray your questions to God and watch how He might reveal Himself to you over the week as you TEND through a few verses or as you reread the book of the Bible. As Jesus said in John 14:26, the Holy Spirit will teach us truth, so give Him the space to do that. But if you have wrestled with the verses and desire further clarification, it can be helpful to open a commentary and see what a scholar on the subject has to say. There is nothing new under the sun, so we can rest assured that you and I will not come up with a "new understanding" of a passage. It is wise to compare our frame of thinking with that of highly educated biblical scholars.
- *Remember that commentaries are not the Word of God but rather the comments of men or women—albeit well-studied people, but people nonetheless.* Because God is God and not someone we can explain or put in a box and His Word is infinite and alive, incredibly intelligent people can have quite opposing interpretations or views. So read commentaries with an open mind, being careful to remember they are not God's inspired Word.

Some commentaries I have found helpful:

- The Bible Project offers video overviews of each book of the Bible, providing a foundation as you begin to get into the details of the verses.
- *The Moody Bible Commentary*, edited by Michael Rydelnik and Michael Vanlaningham
- *The Tony Evans Bible Commentary* by Pastor Tony Evans
- *The Bible Knowledge* commentaries for the Old Testament and New Testament, edited by John F. Walvoord and Roy B. Zuck
- *The IVP Bible Background* commentaries for the Old Testament and New Testament
- The Wiersbe Bible commentaries for the Old Testament and New Testament by beloved scholar Warren Wiersbe
- Bible Hub (http://biblehub.com) also has a list of commentaries from reliable theologians for nearly every book in the Bible, such as *Matthew Henry's Concise Commentary on the Whole Bible*, *Maclaren's Expositions*, and *Barnes' Notes on the Whole Bible*.

Your pastor or trusted teachers can likely refer you to other reliable commentaries as well. The key is for commentaries to be seen as secondary rather than the primary focus of your study.

NOTES

Introduction

1. Michael G. Wechler, "Ruth," in *The Moody Bible Commentary*, ed. Michael Rydelnik and Michael Vanlaningham (Moody Publishers, 2014), 392–93.

Setting the Context

1. Rachel Niemyer, "The Metanarrative of Scripture," Impact 360 Institute, accessed November 13, 2024, https://www.impact360institute.org/articles/the-metanarrative-of-scripture-2/.
2. John W. Reed, "Ruth," in *The Bible Knowledge Commentary: Old Testament*, ed. John F. Walvoord and Roy B. Zuck (Victor Books, 1985), 418.

Week 1 | Returning to God

1. "*Sub*," in *The Complete Word Study Dictionary of the OT: Word Study Series*, ed. Warren Barr Baker and Eugene Carpenter (AMG Publishers, 2003), 1108.
2. "Ruth," in *The Nelson Study Bible: New King James Version*, ed. Earl D. Radmacher, Ronald B. Allen, and H. Wayne House (Thomas Nelson, 1997), 441.
3. "Widow," in *The Holman Bible Dictionary*, ed. Chad Brand, Charles Draper, and Archie England (Holman Reference, 2003), 1671.
4. The Hebrew word transliterated *selah* appears seventy-one times in the book of Psalms. One interpretation of *selah* is that it's a musical term involving a call to pause and reflect.

Week 2 | Learning to Stay

1. Joseph Benson, "Ruth 2:3," in *Joseph Benson's Commentary on the Old and New Testaments*, https://biblehub.com/commentaries/ruth/2-3 .htm.
2. "Gleaning," in *The Holman Bible Dictionary*, 655.
3. Reed, "Ruth," 422.
4. David Camera, "Eating Together," *Table Talk Magazine*, January 2018, https://tabletalkmagazine.com/article/2018/01/eating-together/.
5. "Widow," in *Holman Illustrated Bible Dictionary*, ed. Chad Brand, Eric Mitchell, and Holman Reference Editorial Staff (Holman Bible Publishers, 2015), 1671.
6. John MacArthur, "Ruth 4:6" in *The MacArthur Bible Commentary* (Thomas Nelson, 2005), 296.

Week 3 | An Active Pursuit of Rest

1. Warren W. Wiersbe, "Ruth 3: The Midnight Meeting," in *The Wiersbe Bible Commentary: Old Testament* (David C. Cook, 2007), 486.
2. Wiersbe, "Ruth 3," 486.
3. Wiersbe, "Ruth 3," 487.
4. Wiersbe, "Ruth 3," 487.

Week 4 | Redemption

1. "Ruth 4," in *Ellicott's Commentary for English Readers*, https://biblehub .com/commentaries/ellicott/ruth/4.htm.
2. "Ruth 4:7–8," in *The IVP Bible Background Commentary: Old Testament*, ed. John H. Walton, Victor H. Matthews, and Mark W. Chavalas (IVP Academic, 2000), 280.
3. "Ruth 4:9–10," 280.
4. "Ruth 4:17," 281.

Look for more in the TEND Your Soul Bible Study Series

TEND Your Soul Bible Study Series

Sustained by a
Living Hope

1 PETER

MARIEL DAVENPORT

COMING SPRING 2026

GOD HEARS HER.

Seek and she will find

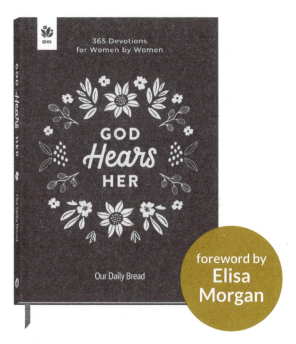

Spread the Word
by Doing One Thing.

- Give a copy of this book as a gift.
- Share the QR code link via your social media.
- Write a review of this book on your blog, favorite bookseller's website, or at ourdailybreadpublishing.org.
- Recommend this book to your church, small group, or book club.

Connect with us. 🅕 🅞

Our Daily Bread Publishing
PO Box 3566, Grand Rapids, MI 49501, USA
Email: books@odbm.org

Love God. Love Others.

with  Our Daily Bread.

Your gift changes lives.

Connect with us. f ⊙

Our Daily Bread Publishing
PO Box 3566, Grand Rapids, MI 49501, USA
Email: books@odbm.org